The Golden Gate Bridge

by Susan Ashley

Reading consultant: Susan Nations, M.Ed., author/literacy coach/consultant

WEEKLY WR READER®
EARLY LEARNING LIBRARY

Please visit our web site at: www.earlyliteracy.cc
For a free color catalog describing Weekly Reader® Early Learning Library's
list of high-quality books, call 1-877-445-5824 (USA) or 1-800-387-3178 (Canada).
Weekly Reader® Early Learning Library's fax: (414) 336-0164.

Library of Congress Cataloging-in-Publication Data

Ashley, Susan.
    The Golden Gate Bridge / by Susan Ashley.
        p. cm. — (Places in American history)
    Includes bibliographical references and index.
    Contents: Reaching across the Gate — Building the Bridge — The Bridge opens —
Longest bridges in the world — Visiting the Bridge.
    ISBN 0-8368-4140-9 (lib. bdg.)
    ISBN 0-8368-4147-6 (softcover)
    1. Golden Gate Bridge (San Francisco, Calif.)—Juvenile literature. [1. Golden Gate Bridge
(San Francisco, Calif.)] I. Title. II. Series.
TG25.S225.A84   2004
624.2'3'0979461—dc22

2003062149

This edition first published in 2004 by
Weekly Reader® Early Learning Library
330 West Olive Street, Suite 100
Milwaukee, WI 53212 USA

Copyright © 2004 by Weekly Reader® Early Learning Library

Editor: JoAnn Early Macken
Art direction, cover and layout design: Tammy Gruenewald
Photo research: Diane Laska-Swanke

Photo credits: Cover, title, p. 20 © James P. Rowan; pp. 4, 6, 11, 16, 17, 19, 21 © Gibson Stock Photography;
p. 5 Kami Koenig/© Weekly Reader Early Learning Library, 2004; p. 7 © Stock Montage, Inc.; pp. 8, 10, 12,
13, 14, 18 Golden Gate Bridge, Highway and Transportation District, San Francisco, CA; p. 9 © Hulton
Archive/Getty Images

Printed in the United States of America

1 2 3 4 5 6 7 8 9 08 07 06 05 04

Table of Contents

The Golden Gate Bridge is a
symbol of San Francisco.

Reaching across the Gate

The Golden Gate Bridge is one of the most
famous bridges in the world. The bridge is in
California. It links the city of San Francisco to
Marin County.

The bridge crosses a narrow body of water called a strait. The strait connects the Pacific Ocean to San Francisco Bay. The strait is called the Golden Gate Strait. It had that name even before the bridge was built.

The Golden Gate Bridge links San Francisco and Marin County.

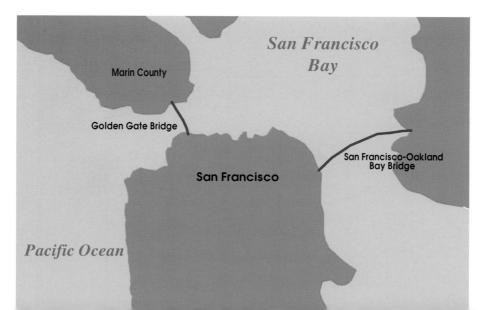

Today, people can take the bridge
or a ferry to get to the city.

Before the bridge was built, people went back
and forth on a ferry. Cars rode on a car ferry.
Sometimes the cars waiting for the ferry lined
up for miles.

Most people thought a bridge was needed. Others did not like the idea. They thought a bridge would spoil the beauty of the bay. They also remembered the earthquake of 1906. Could a bridge survive an earthquake?

Many streets and buildings were destroyed in the 1906 earthquake.

Some people thought that building a bridge across the strait was impossible. They thought the water was too deep. They thought the project was too dangerous. Joseph B. Strauss believed it could be done. Strauss was an engineer. He had built many bridges before.

Joseph B. Strauss worked very hard to build the Golden Gate Bridge.

Strauss could not start the bridge until 1933. The Great Depression struck the country. Many people were out of work. The bridge was built so that people in San Francisco would have jobs.

During the Great Depression, many people lost their jobs and their homes.

Building the Bridge

Building the bridge was dangerous work. The men worked high above the water. Strauss wanted them to be safe. He put safety nets below them, just like circus performers use. The men wore hard hats. Safety belts tied them to the bridge.

The men working on the bridge had to be careful.

The Golden Gate Bridge is a suspension bridge. Two thick overhead cables hold up the roadway. Two towers hold up the cables. Long wire ropes connect the roadway to the cables. At both ends of the bridge, the cables are attached to huge blocks of concrete. The blocks are called anchorages.

This view of the bridge shows the towers, the cables, and the wire ropes that hold up the roadway.

The tower on the right was built first. The tower on the left took longer to build because it was standing in deep water.

Workers on the Golden Gate Bridge built the anchorages first. The towers were next, and then the cables. The cables must be very strong. They are more than 3 feet (almost 1 meter) thick.

The workers built the roadway last. The men worked in teams. They started at the towers and worked outward. Each team had to work at the same speed to keep the bridge balanced. At times, the roadway seemed to hang in midair.

Parts of the roadway had to be joined together.

The Bridge Opens

The bridge was finished in 1937. On May 27, crowds of people walked across it. The next day, the bridge opened to cars. The entire city celebrated. Church bells rang. Foghorns bellowed. Boats filled the bay, and planes flew overhead.

Thousands of people walked across the bridge when it opened.

When the Golden Gate Bridge opened, it was the longest bridge in the world. It was more than 1 mile (1.6 kilometers) long. It is still one of the longest bridges in the world. Its total length is the third longest in the United States.

Longest Bridges in the World

Name of bridge	Location	Total Length	
		Feet	Meters
Storebaelt	Denmark	22,277	6,790
Mackinac	Michigan	18,615	5,674
Verrazano-Narrows	New York	13,700	4,176
Akashi Kaikyo	Japan	12,828	3,910
Golden Gate	California	8,981	2,737

Large ships can pass beneath the bridge.

The bridge is high as well as long. At the middle, the roadway is 220 feet (67 m) above the water. Tall ships can pass beneath it. The bridge is sturdy enough to survive strong earthquakes. It can stand winds up to 100 miles (161 km) per hour. In strong winds, the bridge can sway as much as 27 feet (8 m).

The Golden Gate Bridge is famous for its color. Most bridges built at that time were painted black or gray. Some people wanted to paint the bridge gold to match its name. The builders chose orange to blend in with the hills and the city. The paint protects the bridge from the salty ocean air.

The bridge is painted bright orange.

The Golden Gate Bridge celebrated its fiftieth anniversary on May 24, 1987. More than two hundred thousand people walked across the bridge that day. Marching bands joined them. The bridge's two towers were lit up for the first time.

People in San Francisco celebrated the bridge's fiftieth birthday.

Visiting the Bridge

Today, people walk, ride bikes, and drive cars across the bridge. Iron workers and toll takers work on the bridge. Painters fix peeling paint. Inspectors climb up the towers. They look for problems along the cables.

Thousands of cars cross the bridge every day.

A statue of Joseph B. Strauss stands near the bridge. Strauss once said, "Do not be afraid to dream." Building the Golden Gate Bridge was his dream. People told him that it could not be done. He proved it was possible.

A statue of Joseph B. Strauss stands at one end of the bridge.

The Golden Gate Bridge is more than a bridge. It is a symbol of San Francisco. It is a monument to the people who built it. All Americans can be proud of this amazing landmark.

The Golden Gate Bridge is a beautiful landmark.

Glossary

anchorage — a large block of concrete that holds the ends of a bridge's cables in place

anniversary — the date that something special happened

bellow — to make a deep, loud sound

cable — a thick, strong rope made of wire

engineer — a person who designs or builds bridges, buildings, or machines

ferry — a boat that carries people and cars

Great Depression — a period in American history when many people had no jobs

impossible — not able to be done

inspector — someone who checks things and looks for problems

landmark — an important object or building

roadway — the part of a bridge that cars travel on

For More Information

Books

Kaner, Etta. *Bridges*. Kids Can Press, 1997.

Nelson, Sharlene and Ted Nelson. *The Golden Gate Bridge*. Danbury, Conn.: Children's Press, 2001.

Owens, Thomas S. and T. O. Owens. *The Golden Gate Bridge*. New York: Powerkids Press, 2001.

Sturges, Philemon. *Bridges Are to Cross*. Puffin Books, 2000.

Web Sites

Welcome to Golden Gate Bridge, Highway and Transportation District

www.goldengate.org

The bridge's official web site

Wonders of the World Data Bank

www.pbs.org/wgbh/buildingbig/wonder/structure/golden_gate.html

Golden Gate Bridge history and facts

Index

About the Author

Susan Ashley has written over eighteen books for children, including two picture books about dogs, *Puppy Love* and *When I'm Happy, I Smile*. She enjoys animals and writing about them. Susan lives in Wisconsin with her husband and two frisky felines.